Maximize Yourself Through Manifestation

Manifestation Journal

APRIL LOVE

outskirts
press

Maximize Yourself Through Manifestation
Manifestation Journal
All Rights Reserved.
Copyright © 2022 April Love
v1.0

The opinions expressed in this manuscript are solely the opinions of the author and do not represent the opinions or thoughts of the publisher. The author has represented and warranted full ownership and/or legal right to publish all the materials in this book.

This book may not be reproduced, transmitted, or stored in whole or in part by any means, including graphic, electronic, or mechanical without the express written consent of the publisher except in the case of brief quotations embodied in critical articles and reviews.

Outskirts Press, Inc.
http://www.outskirtspress.com

ISBN: 978-1-9772-5450-4

Outskirts Press and the "OP" logo are trademarks belonging to Outskirts Press, Inc.

PRINTED IN THE UNITED STATES OF AMERICA

The reason I decided to write this guide is because Manifestation, Visualization, Law of Attraction and Affirmations has worked for me. The biggest manifestation that has happened in my life so far has been when I conceived our child. Just to give you a little background I wanted a child on and off for years starting in my 20's. Long story short I never got pregnant before my practice of manifestation. I tried In Vitro Fertilization (IVF) but without Law of Attraction, without Visualization, without Affirmations and, without Manifestation. When women are trying to Conceive (TTC) and have problems they usually read up on all the things they should do for their body. What foods to eat, how to take care of yourself, but no one tells you how to mentally have control over your life with your mind and the way you think. Manifestation has also worked for me in many other ways including jobs and money. The key is you must make yourself believe and you also must put in some work. Fast forward to when getting pregnant worked with manifestation and law of attraction we conceived the first time this time. I started manifesting a year before we started but the last 30 days before the procedure I did it consistently. Manifestation can work for you if you give it time and put in the work and believe. You can use this guide for anything that you want to manifest i.e. job, career, love life, money. I will be referring to my conception journey just because it was the most meaningful one for me. You can apply these tools to whatever you want to manifest.

1.
How to Make Manifestation Work for You

YOU MAY HAVE heard of Law of Attraction, Manifestation, Affirmations or Visualization. That is what this book is all about. The reason I wanted to share this with others is because I have tried these things for many years. My only problem was consistency I noticed that if I were not consistent, things would not happen as much as they would if I were consistent. When I was very consistent things happened for sure. I want to tell you how this works and how it has worked for me. No matter what religion you are or are not, there is a belief for many, that what you think so it is(good or bad). I have put this to the test many times. This is not an easy thing to do but it is doable. We must first change the way we think. Some of the things that you say to yourself you yourself will not believe them but over time you will start to believe them to be true.

The first step is for the next seven days (start today) every time you have a bad thought about yourself, immediately replace it with a new one. i.e. "I am so lazy for missing my workout today" replace it with

Maximize Yourself Through Manifestation

"Tomorrow my body will be recharged enough for a great workout". You must get control of your thoughts. Do not let your thoughts have control over you! They have been in charge for long enough. Once the week is up come back to the journal for the next step. Good Luck! Return date_____

How did you do?

_____
_____
_____
_____

Was it hard for you to replace your thoughts?

_____
_____
_____
_____
_____

Continue to practice changing the way you think. It makes a difference when it comes to manifesting the things you want in your life. The next step is to come up with one thing that you genuinely want to achieve or have happen in your life. Really think about it and make sure it is something that you want to achieve or happen soon. The longer goals will come later. List the one thing below.

1. _____
_____
_____
_____
_____

Manifestation Journal

This is where the work comes in. For the next 30 days you need to write down these things you want to happen. This can be a paragraph. You can write something different everyday or the same statement over and over, but it must be for 30 consecutive days. If you miss a day, 30 days must start over (you may use the 30-day section in this journal at this point). I will share with you one of my paragraphs I wrote months before I conceived our child. As I mentioned before I have never been pregnant and at this time in my life I thought I was incapable of becoming pregnant. I did not believe what I was writing when I wrote it the first day maybe up until the 25th day but on one of those days my mind started believing it.

16July2019 "We will have a successful In Vitro Fertilization (IVF) cycle the first time. We will have a healthy baby with no mental problems and no disabilities. I will nurture my womb so that it is healthy and will carry with no complications. I will have a healthy pregnancy and will experience no mental instabilities during or after I give birth." I then started to write it down every single day. I will share that at the end of each time I wrote my affirmation I added "Thank you Universe, Thank you God". I personally believe in a higher power, but it is up to you and what you believe. This is your journey; I am merely a spark of an idea for your thoughts.

I got pregnant with my first child January 2020 (It was a long process). We were on a waiting list for the Invitro Fertilization (IVF) cycle and got the call to start in October 2019. Your statement does not have to be this long it can be as short as you want but be awfully specific. One thing I did not mention in this one above was dates. If I had mentioned dates like I did in others I have done I probably would have got the call sooner. Nonetheless, I am still happy it happened when it did. I have done manifestation practices with getting a job position, promotions, having a certain amount of money in my bank account, having the right people around me, finding my 'tribe' etc. You name it I probably manifested it. Let us move on to visualization which essentially

3

ties up with manifestation, law of attraction and affirmations.

1. Visualization

Visualization is a mental visual image of something. When manifesting anything in your life you must be able to see it. One of the things you can do is create a vision board. It is quite simple to create a vision board. You can get a small or large poster board or any type of background paper for that matter. Grab some old magazines, markers, and scissors. Then make a list of the thing or things you want to achieve below or on another piece of paper (it can be only 1 thing; it does not have to be many things). Then go through the magazine and look for a thing or things that relate to what you want to achieve. The reason you should make a list of the things you want to achieve is just so you have an idea of your focus. If you see something in the magazine that resonates with you, use it. You do not have to stick to that list. If you do not do the magazine route you can also just write the words down (writing things down for some reason makes things happen). The whole idea is creating something that you can see every day and reflect on every day. Once your mind can see the thing you want it communicates with the universe exactly what it is you want. Practicing visualization is training your mind to see the things you want and to know that these things are possible for you. I noticed the more I wrote down or saw with my eyes more of those things would happen. It is a message. It is energy!

_____
_____
_____
_____
_____
_____

2. Law of Attraction

Let us talk about Law of Attraction. I heard of Law of Attraction from time to time over my adult years but never really got into what it was. One day I was told about this movie call "The Secret". At the time I had just returned from overseas from a deployment and I was living with my friend at the time. So, I got bored one night and said I want to watch this movie. It went over how Law of Attraction works and how you create Law of Attraction everyday and may not even realize it. What happens is based on your frequency and vibration (because we are all energy, right?) you attract what you give out. You attract what you think. You attract that same frequency and vibration that you are projecting. For instance, if you are constantly thinking negative thoughts and bad things most likely you have bad days and bad things happen. If you think positive things and good things, you have more good days and good things usually happen. Have you ever thought about someone and thought about them again and they are on your mind and that day or a couple of days go by and that exact person contacts you or you see this person unexpectedly? This is Law of Attraction. Do it. Purposely think of someone that is living, over and over and see will you cross paths somehow. I have tested this theory many times and it works every time. A few times I have thought someone up that I really did not care to contact me, and they did. So be careful! Working on your positive thinking increases your frequency with the universe and when your frequency is higher the more connected you are and the more it works in your favor.

Are your thoughts mostly negative or positive?

_____
_____
_____

Maximize Yourself Through Manifestation

Let us test this theory. For the next couple of days before you move to the next section. Do your best to think of only positive thoughts. When something negative comes to your mind acknowledge it. Give it a second and replace the thought with a positive one. A positive one, on purpose. After each day come back and record how the positive thinking went for you. As you may notice, we already tried this with manifestation. Law of Attraction is simply the same. It takes lots of practice.

How did it go today?

_____
_____
_____
_____
_____
_____

Continue for the next few days and record your thoughts daily.

_____
_____
_____
_____
_____
_____
_____
_____
_____
_____
_____

Manifestation Journal

_____

_____
_____
_____
_____
_____
_____
_____
_____
_____
_____
_____
_____
_____
_____
_____
_____

I want to be truly clear, when we a speaking of Manifestation, Visualization, Affirmations and Law of Attraction. If you believe in a higher power, a creator (which I do) this does not take away from your creator. This is showing you power was also given to you. Power was always in you. You have the power. Now that that is clear let us practice some more. Have you ever spoken positive words to yourself? Have you ever looked in the mirror into your face, into your eyes and told yourself "You can do this!" "You've got this!" "You are worthy." These are Affirmation but they are usually done with 1st person. "I AM." These are two immensely powerful words. When practicing affirmations at first just like with the manifestation journal you may not believe what you are saying but repeating these over and over for at least 21 days you will start to believe what is already true. The goal of it all is to be the highest you that you can be. To operate at the highest frequency as you possibly can. That is the goal!

List some "I AM" affirmations below that you believe or want to believe about yourself. (Ex. I AM powerful. I AM a successful. I AM a kind human. I AM worthy etc.)

_____
_____
_____
_____
_____
_____
_____
_____
_____
_____
_____
_____
_____
_____
_____
_____
_____
_____
_____
_____
_____
_____

The remaining of this book is dedicated to you. You have the foundation now let us continue the work.

(Day 1) Today's Date_____

Were your thoughts positive today? If not, how could you have replaced the negative thought?

_____
_____
_____
_____
_____
_____
_____
_____
_____

What is your manifestation affirmation today?

_____
_____
_____
_____
_____
_____
_____
_____
_____

Maximize Yourself Through Manifestation

What do you want to attract into your life tomorrow?
_____
_____
_____
_____
_____
_____
_____
_____
_____

I AM
_____
_____
_____
_____

Manifestation Journal

(Day 2) Today's Date_____

Were your thoughts positive today? If not, how could you have replaced the negative thought?

_____
_____
_____
_____
_____
_____
_____
_____
_____
_____

What is your manifestation affirmation today?

_____
_____
_____
_____
_____
_____
_____
_____
_____
_____

Maximize Yourself Through Manifestation

What do you want to attract into your life tomorrow?
_____
_____
_____
_____
_____
_____
_____
_____
_____

I AM
_____
_____
_____
_____

Manifestation Journal

(Day 3) Today's Date_____

Were your thoughts positive today? If not, how could you have replaced the negative thought?

_____
_____
_____
_____
_____
_____
_____
_____
_____

What is your manifestation affirmation today?

_____
_____
_____
_____
_____
_____
_____
_____
_____

Maximize Yourself Through Manifestation

What do you want to attract into your life tomorrow?

_____
_____
_____
_____
_____
_____
_____
_____
_____

I AM
_____
_____
_____
_____

Manifestation Journal

(Day 4) Today's Date_____

Were your thoughts positive today? If not, how could you have replaced the negative thought?

_____
_____
_____
_____
_____
_____
_____
_____
_____

What is your manifestation affirmation today?

_____
_____
_____
_____
_____
_____
_____
_____
_____

Maximize Yourself Through Manifestation

What do you want to attract into your life tomorrow?
_____
_____
_____
_____
_____
_____
_____
_____
_____

I AM
_____
_____
_____
_____
_____

Manifestation Journal

(Day 5) Today's Date_____

Were your thoughts positive today? If not, how could you have replaced the negative thought?

_____
_____
_____
_____
_____
_____
_____
_____

What is your manifestation affirmation today?

_____
_____
_____
_____
_____
_____
_____
_____

Maximize Yourself Through Manifestation

What do you want to attract into your life tomorrow?
_____
_____
_____
_____
_____
_____
_____
_____
_____

I AM
_____
_____
_____
_____
_____

Manifestation Journal

(Day 6) Today's Date_____

Were your thoughts positive today? If not, how could you have replaced the negative thought?

_____
_____
_____
_____
_____
_____
_____
_____
_____
_____

What is your manifestation affirmation today?

_____
_____
_____
_____
_____
_____
_____
_____
_____
_____

Maximize Yourself Through Manifestation

What do you want to attract into your life tomorrow?
___
___
___
___
___
___
___
___
___

I AM
___
___
___
___

Manifestation Journal

(Day 7) Today's Date_____

Were your thoughts positive today? If not, how could you have replaced the negative thought?

_____
_____
_____
_____
_____
_____
_____
_____
_____

What is your manifestation affirmation today?

_____
_____
_____
_____
_____
_____
_____
_____
_____

What do you want to attract into your life tomorrow?
_____
_____
_____
_____
_____
_____
_____
_____
_____

I AM
_____
_____
_____
_____
_____

Manifestation Journal

(Day 8) Today's Date_____

Were your thoughts positive today? If not, how could you have replaced the negative thought?

_____
_____
_____
_____
_____
_____
_____
_____
_____
_____

What is your manifestation affirmation today?

_____
_____
_____
_____
_____
_____
_____
_____
_____
_____

Maximize Yourself Through Manifestation

What do you want to attract into your life tomorrow?
_____
_____
_____
_____
_____
_____
_____
_____
_____

I AM
_____
_____
_____
_____
_____

Manifestation Journal

(Day 9) Today's Date_____

Were your thoughts positive today? If not, how could you have replaced the negative thought?

_____
_____
_____
_____
_____
_____
_____
_____
_____
_____

What is your manifestation affirmation today?

_____
_____
_____
_____
_____
_____
_____
_____
_____
_____

Maximize Yourself Through Manifestation

What do you want to attract into your life tomorrow?
_____
_____
_____
_____
_____
_____
_____
_____
_____

I AM
_____
_____
_____
_____
_____

(Day 10) Today's Date_____

Were your thoughts positive today? If not, how could you have replaced the negative thought?

_____
_____
_____
_____
_____
_____
_____
_____
_____
_____

What is your manifestation affirmation today?

_____
_____
_____
_____
_____
_____
_____
_____
_____
_____

What do you want to attract into your life tomorrow?
___
___
___
___
___
___
___
___

I AM
___
___
___
___

Manifestation Journal

(Day 11) Today's Date_____

Were your thoughts positive today? If not, how could you have replaced the negative thought?

_____
_____
_____
_____
_____
_____
_____
_____
_____
_____

What is your manifestation affirmation today?

_____
_____
_____
_____
_____
_____
_____
_____
_____

Maximize Yourself Through Manifestation

What do you want to attract into your life tomorrow?
_____
_____
_____
_____
_____
_____
_____
_____
_____

I AM
_____
_____
_____
_____

(Day 12) Today's Date_____

Were your thoughts positive today? If not, how could you have replaced the negative thought?

_____
_____
_____
_____
_____
_____
_____
_____
_____
_____

What is your manifestation affirmation today?

_____
_____
_____
_____
_____
_____
_____
_____
_____
_____

Maximize Yourself Through Manifestation

What do you want to attract into your life tomorrow?
_____
_____
_____
_____
_____
_____
_____
_____
_____

I AM
_____
_____
_____
_____

Manifestation Journal

(Day 13) Today's Date_____

Were your thoughts positive today? If not, how could you have replaced the negative thought?

_____
_____
_____
_____
_____
_____
_____
_____
_____

What is your manifestation affirmation today?

_____
_____
_____
_____
_____
_____
_____
_____
_____

Maximize Yourself Through Manifestation

What do you want to attract into your life tomorrow?
_____
_____
_____
_____
_____
_____
_____
_____
_____

I AM
_____
_____
_____
_____

Manifestation Journal

(Day 14) Today's Date_____

Were your thoughts positive today? If not, how could you have replaced the negative thought?

_____
_____
_____
_____
_____
_____
_____
_____
_____

What is your manifestation affirmation today?

_____
_____
_____
_____
_____
_____
_____
_____
_____

What do you want to attract into your life tomorrow?
_____
_____
_____
_____
_____
_____
_____
_____

I AM
_____
_____
_____
_____

(Day 15) Today's Date_____

Were your thoughts positive today? If not, how could you have replaced the negative thought?

_____
_____
_____
_____
_____
_____
_____
_____
_____

What is your manifestation affirmation today?

_____
_____
_____
_____
_____
_____
_____
_____
_____

What do you want to attract into your life tomorrow?
___
___
___
___
___
___
___
___
___
___

I AM
___
___
___
___

(Day 16) Today's Date_____

Were your thoughts positive today? If not, how could you have replaced the negative thought?

_____
_____
_____
_____
_____
_____
_____
_____
_____

What is your manifestation affirmation today?

_____
_____
_____
_____
_____
_____
_____
_____
_____

Maximize Yourself Through Manifestation

What do you want to attract into your life tomorrow?
_____
_____
_____
_____
_____
_____
_____
_____
_____

I AM
_____
_____
_____
_____

Manifestation Journal

(Day 17) Today's Date_____

Were your thoughts positive today? If not, how could you have replaced the negative thought?

_____
_____
_____
_____
_____
_____
_____
_____
_____

What is your manifestation affirmation today?

_____
_____
_____
_____
_____
_____
_____
_____
_____

Maximize Yourself Through Manifestation

What do you want to attract into your life tomorrow?
_____
_____
_____
_____
_____
_____
_____
_____

I AM
_____
_____
_____
_____

(Day 18) Today's Date_____

Were your thoughts positive today? If not, how could you have replaced the negative thought?

_____
_____
_____
_____
_____
_____
_____
_____
_____
_____

What is your manifestation affirmation today?

_____
_____
_____
_____
_____
_____
_____
_____
_____
_____

What do you want to attract into your life tomorrow?
___
___
___
___
___
___
___
___
___
___

I AM
___
___
___
___

Manifestation Journal

(Day 19) Today's Date_____

Were your thoughts positive today? If not, how could you have replaced the negative thought?

_____
_____
_____
_____
_____
_____
_____
_____
_____
_____

What is your manifestation affirmation today?

_____
_____
_____
_____
_____
_____
_____
_____
_____
_____

Maximize Yourself Through Manifestation

What do you want to attract into your life tomorrow?

_____
_____
_____
_____
_____
_____
_____
_____
_____

I AM

_____
_____
_____
_____
_____

Manifestation Journal

(Day 20) Today's Date_____

Were your thoughts positive today? If not, how could you have replaced the negative thought?

_____
_____
_____
_____
_____
_____
_____
_____
_____

What is your manifestation affirmation today?

_____
_____
_____
_____
_____
_____
_____
_____
_____

Maximize Yourself Through Manifestation

What do you want to attract into your life tomorrow?
_____
_____
_____
_____
_____
_____
_____
_____
_____

I AM
_____
_____
_____
_____

(Day 21) Today's Date_____

Were your thoughts positive today? If not, how could you have replaced the negative thought?

_____
_____
_____
_____
_____
_____
_____
_____

What is your manifestation affirmation today?

_____
_____
_____
_____
_____
_____
_____
_____

Maximize Yourself Through Manifestation

What do you want to attract into your life tomorrow?
_____
_____
_____
_____
_____
_____
_____
_____
_____

I AM
_____
_____
_____
_____
_____

Manifestation Journal

(Day 22) Today's Date_____

Were your thoughts positive today? If not, how could you have replaced the negative thought?

_____
_____
_____
_____
_____
_____
_____
_____
_____

What is your manifestation affirmation today?

_____
_____
_____
_____
_____
_____
_____
_____
_____

Maximize Yourself Through Manifestation

What do you want to attract into your life tomorrow?
_____
_____
_____
_____
_____
_____
_____
_____
_____

I AM
_____
_____
_____
_____
_____

Manifestation Journal

(Day 23) Today's Date

Were your thoughts positive today? If not, how could you have replaced the negative thought?

_____
_____
_____
_____
_____
_____
_____
_____

What is your manifestation affirmation today?

_____
_____
_____
_____
_____
_____
_____
_____

Maximize Yourself Through Manifestation

What do you want to attract into your life tomorrow?
___
___
___
___
___
___
___
___
___

I AM
___
___
___
___

Manifestation Journal

(Day 24) Today's Date

Were your thoughts positive today? If not, how could you have replaced the negative thought?

_____
_____
_____
_____
_____
_____
_____
_____

What is your manifestation affirmation today?

_____
_____
_____
_____
_____
_____
_____
_____

Maximize Yourself Through Manifestation

What do you want to attract into your life tomorrow?

_____
_____
_____
_____
_____
_____
_____
_____
_____

I AM

_____
_____
_____
_____

Manifestation Journal

(Day 25) Today's Date_____

Were your thoughts positive today? If not, how could you have replaced the negative thought?

_____
_____
_____
_____
_____
_____
_____
_____
_____

What is your manifestation affirmation today?

_____
_____
_____
_____
_____
_____
_____
_____
_____

Maximize Yourself Through Manifestation

What do you want to attract into your life tomorrow?
_____
_____
_____
_____
_____
_____
_____
_____
_____

I AM
_____
_____
_____
_____

Manifestation Journal

(Day 26) Today's Date _____

Were your thoughts positive today? If not, how could you have replaced the negative thought?

_____
_____
_____
_____
_____
_____
_____
_____
_____
_____

What is your manifestation affirmation today?

_____
_____
_____
_____
_____
_____
_____
_____
_____
_____

Maximize Yourself Through Manifestation

What do you want to attract into your life tomorrow?

_____
_____
_____
_____
_____
_____
_____
_____
_____

I AM

_____
_____
_____
_____

Manifestation Journal

(Day 27) Today's Date_____   _____

Were your thoughts positive today? If not, how could you have replaced the negative thought?

_____
_____
_____
_____
_____
_____
_____
_____
_____

What is your manifestation affirmation today?

_____
_____
_____
_____
_____
_____
_____
_____
_____

Maximize Yourself Through Manifestation

What do you want to attract into your life tomorrow?
_____
_____
_____
_____
_____
_____
_____
_____
_____

I AM
_____
_____
_____
_____

(Day 28) Today's Date _____

Were your thoughts positive today? If not, how could you have replaced the negative thought?

_____
_____
_____
_____
_____
_____
_____
_____
_____

What is your manifestation affirmation today?

_____
_____
_____
_____
_____
_____
_____
_____
_____

Maximize Yourself Through Manifestation

What do you want to attract into your life tomorrow?
___
___
___
___
___
___
___
___

I AM
___
___
___
___

Manifestation Journal

(Day 29) Today's Date

Were your thoughts positive today? If not, how could you have replaced the negative thought?

_____
_____
_____
_____
_____
_____
_____
_____
_____
_____

What is your manifestation affirmation today?

_____
_____
_____
_____
_____
_____
_____
_____
_____
_____

Maximize Yourself Through Manifestation

What do you want to attract into your life tomorrow?
_____
_____
_____
_____
_____
_____
_____
_____
_____

I AM
_____
_____
_____
_____

Manifestation Journal

(Day 30) Today's Date _____

Were your thoughts positive today? If not, how could you have replaced the negative thought?

_____
_____
_____
_____
_____
_____
_____
_____
_____

What is your manifestation affirmation today?

_____
_____
_____
_____
_____
_____
_____
_____
_____

Maximize Yourself Through Manifestation

What do you want to attract into your life tomorrow?
_____
_____
_____
_____
_____
_____
_____
_____
_____
_____

I AM
_____
_____
_____
_____
_____

Cheat Codes

IS THERE SOMEONE you have a problem with that you just do not get along with or does not like you for whatever reason and you cannot get along with?

Cheat Code: Send positive energy to this person every day. This is extremely hard if you don't like the person but if you have to be in this person life whether it's a coworker or family member then you might as well make it better through your positive energy.

My example: Me and my co-worker were not getting along. I absolutely could not be in the same room as this person to share the same air. Everyday I sent a positive thought his way. I asked the Universe to bless him and keep him safe. About 1 month to a month and half I started noticing his attitude change towards me. He would smile and was much nicer. I am not sure if I changed or he changed but someone changed, and it made the workplace less hostile.

Do you feel you need your day to run a little smoother or that you need some control of your day?

Cheat Code: I have found that creating a morning routine works wonders. If you have children, you must wake up 30 minutes to an hour before them to get started. Same with a career or job. If you must wake up a few minutes early that is the sacrifice, but it will be all worth it. A morning routine helps to keep you balanced and give you a sense that you are in control of your day.

My Example: My morning routine used to be 1 hour, but I found that did not work for me, so I cut it down to 30 minutes a day. I was doing to get a full yoga class in my morning routine but saw that does not work. I decided if I must time to work out later, I will do a full class or full workout then. My morning routine consist of Sun Salutation A x 5, Sun Salutation B x 3 which takes about 10-minute, 10 minutes meditation and then I write in both my manifestation journals which takes about 5 minutes each. I thought my 10 minutes meditation was too short, but the reality is when you are doing yoga it is also a form of meditation. If I have more time I do more.

Do you sometimes complete your day and the task or tasks you thought of doing that day has been pushed to the next day?
Cheat Code: Make a to-do list at the beginning of your day. When you write down things that needs to be done, they tend to get done even when you forget about the list. Its energy put out into the Universe.
My Example: When I do not write things down, things do not get done. When I do things get done whether it is because of the energy put out or because I feel the obligation to get it done sets in.

About the Author

APRIL LOVE IS a 40-year-old from Columbus, GA. She lives in Las Vegas with her wife and sonshine and her 2 poodles. She is a U.S Air Force Veteran and a 200 hr registered Yoga Instructor. She has a degree in Nutrition and a degree in Business. She has been living a holistic lifestyle since 2016. She has been practicing manifestation, law of attraction, visualization, and affirmations since 2018. Once she started practicing consistently, she noticed all things falling into place in her life. At one time it was unbelievable to see all the things on her vision board come to life one at a time.